A Miscellany of Poems

By

G. K. Chesterton

British Library Cataloguing-in-Publication Data
A catalogue record for this book is available from the
British Library

G. K. Chesterton

Gilbert Keith Chesterton was born in London in 1874. He studied at the Slade School of Art, and upon graduating began to work as a freelance journalist. By 1905, he had a regular and popular column with the Illustrated London News, and began to write on an array of topics. Over the course of his life, his literary output was incredibly diverse and highly prolific, ranging from philosophy and ontology to art criticism and detective fiction. However, he is probably best-remembered for his Christian apologetics, most notably in Orthodoxy (1908) and The Everlasting Man (1925). George Bernard Shaw dubbed Chesterton "a man of colossal genius," and of his fiction Argentine author Jorge Luis Borges said "Chesterton knew how to make the most of a detective story." Chesterton died in 1936, aged 62.

Alliterativism (1914)

French airmen have been flying over Baden and Bavaria, violating Belgian neutrality -Stated on German authority in the Westminster Gazette

See the flying French depart
Like the bees of Bonaparte,
Swarming up with a most venomous vitality.
Over Baden and Bavaria,
And Brighton and Bulgaria,
Thus violating Belgian neutrality.

And the injured Prussian may
Not unreasonably say
"Why, it cannot be so small a nationality
Since Brixton and Batavia,
Bolivia and Belgravia,
Are bursting with the Belgian neutrality."

By pure Alliteration
You may trace this curious nation,
And respect this somewhat scattered Principality;
When you see a B in Both
You may take your Bible oath
You are violating Belgian neutrality.

Americanisation

Britannia needs no Boulevards,
    No spaces wide and gay:
Her march was through the crooked streets
    Along the narrow way.
Nor looks she where, New York's seduction,
The Broadway leadeth to destruction.

Britannia needs no Cafes:
    If Coffee needs must be,
Its place should be the Coffee-house
    Where Johnson growled for Tea;
But who can hear that human mountain
Growl for an ice-cream soda-fountain?

She needs no Russian Theatre
    Where Father strangles Mother,
In scenes where all the characters
    And colours kill each other--
Her boast is freedom had by halves,
And Britons never shall be Slavs.

But if not hers the Dance of Death,
    Great Dostoievsky's dance,
And if the things most finely French
    Are better done in France--

Might not Americanisation
Be best applied to its own nation?

Ere every shop shall be a store
    And every Trade a Trust . . .
Lo, many men in many lands
    Know when their cause is just.
There will be quite a large attendance
When we Declare our Independence.

Antichrist, or the Reunion of Christendom: An Ode

"A Bill which has shocked the conscience of every Christian community in Europe."-Mr. F. E. Smith, on the Welsh Disestablishment Bill.

Are they clinging to their crosses,
F. E. Smith,
Where the Breton boat-fleet tosses,
Are they, Smith?
Do they, fasting, trembling, bleeding,
Wait the news from this our city?
Groaning "That's the Second Reading!"
Hissing "There is still Committee!"
If the voice of Cecil falters,
If McKenna's point has pith,
Do they tremble for their altars?
Do they, Smith?

Russian peasants round their pope
Huddled, Smith,
Hear about it all, I hope,
Don't they, Smith?
In the mountain hamlets clothing
Peaks beyond Caucasian pales,
Where Establishment means nothing
And they never heard of Wales,
Do they read it all in Hansard -
With a crib to read it with -

"Welsh Tithes: Dr. Clifford answered."
Really, Smith?

In the lands where Christians were,
F. E. Smith,
In the little lands laid bare,
Smith, O Smith!
Where the Turkish bands are busy
And the Tory name is blessed
Since they hailed the Cross of Dizzy
On the banners from the West!
Men don't think it half so hard if
Islam burns their kin and kith,
Since a curate lives in Cardiff
Saved by Smith.

It would greatly, I must own,
Soothe me, Smith!
If you left this theme alone,
Holy Smith!
For your legal cause or civil
You fight well and get your fee;
For your God or dream or devil
You will answer, not to me.
Talk about the pews and steeples
And the cash that goes therewith!
But the souls of Christian peoples...
Chuck it, Smith!

The Aristocrat

The Devil is a gentleman, and asks you down to stay
At his little place at What'sitsname (it isn't far away).
They say the sport is splendid; there is always something new,
And fairy scenes, and fearful feats that none but he can do;
He can shoot the feathered cherubs if they fly on the estate,
Or fish for Father Neptune with the mermaids for a bait;
He scaled amid the staggering stars that precipice, the sky,
And blew his trumpet above heaven, and got by mastery
The starry crown of God Himself, and shoved it on the shelf;
But the Devil is a gentleman, and doesn't brag himself.

O blind your eyes and break your heart and hack your hand away,
And lose your love and shave your head; but do not go to stay
At the little place in What'sitsname where folks are rich and clever;
The golden and the goodly house, where things grow worse for ever;
There are things you need not know of, though you live and die in vain,

There are souls more sick of pleasure than you are sick of pain;
There is a game of April Fool that's played behind its door,
Where the fool remains for ever and the April comes no more,
Where the splendour of the daylight grows drearier than the dark,
And life droops like a vulture that once was such a lark:
And that is the Blue Devil that once was the Blue Bird;
For the Devil is a gentleman, and doesn't keep his word.

A Ballad of Abbreviations

The American's a hustler, for he says so,
  And surely the American must know.
He will prove to you with figures why it pays so
  Beginning with his boyhood long ago.
When the slow-maturing anecdote is ripest,
  He'll dictate it like a Board of Trade Report,
And because he has no time to call a typist,
  He calls her a Stenographer for short.

He is never known to loiter or malinger,
  He rushes, for he knows he has "a date" ;
He is always on the spot and full of ginger,
  Which is why he is invariably late.
When he guesses that it's getting even later,
  His vocabulary's vehement and swift,
And he yells for what he calls the Elevator,
  A slang abbreviation for a lift.

Then nothing can be nattier or nicer
  For those who like a light and rapid style.
Than to trifle with a work of Mr Dreiser
  As it comes along in waggons by the mile.
He has taught us what a swift selective art meant
  By description of his dinners and all that,
And his dwelling, which he says is an Apartment,
  Because he cannot stop to say a flat.

We may whisper of his wild precipitation,
  That it's speed in rather longer than a span,
But there really is a definite occasion
  When he does not use the longest word he can.
When he substitutes, I freely make admission,
  One shorter and much easier to spell;
If you ask him what he thinks of Prohibition,
  He may tell you quite succinctly it is Hell.

A Ballade of an Anti-puritan

They spoke of Progress spiring round,
Of light and Mrs Humphrey Ward -
It is not true to say I frowned,
Or ran about the room and roared;
I might have simply sat and snored -
I rose politely in the club
And said, 'I feel a little bored;
Will someone take me to a pub?'

The new world's wisest did surround
Me; and it pains me to record
I did not think their views profound,
Or their conclusions well assured;
The simple life I can't afford,
Besides, I do not like the grub -
I want a mash and sausage, 'scored' -
Will someone take me to a pub?

I know where Men can still be found,
Anger and clamorous accord,
And virtues growing from the ground,
And fellowship of beer and board,
And song, that is a sturdy cord,
And hope, that is a hardy shrub,
And goodness, that is God's last word -
Will someone take me to a pub?

Envoi

Prince, Bayard would have smashed his sword
To see the sort of knights you dub -
Is that the last of them - O Lord
Will someone take me to a pub?

A Ballade of Suicide (1915)

The gallows in my garden, people say,
Is new and neat and adequately tall;
I tie the noose on in a knowing way
As one that knots his necktie for a ball;
But just as all the neighbours--on the wall--
Are drawing a long breath to shout "Hurray!"
The strangest whim has seized me. . . . After all
I think I will not hang myself to-day.

To-morrow is the time I get my pay--
My uncle's sword is hanging in the hall--
I see a little cloud all pink and grey--
Perhaps the rector's mother will not call--
I fancy that I heard from Mr. Gall
That mushrooms could be cooked another way--
I never read the works of Juvenal--
I think I will not hang myself to-day.

The world will have another washing-day;
The decadents decay; the pedants pall;
And H.G. Wells has found that children play,
And Bernard Shaw discovered that they squall,
Rationalists are growing rational--
And through thick woods one finds a stream astray
So secret that the very sky seems small--
I think I will not hang myself to-day.

ENVOI

Prince, I can hear the trumpet of Germinal,
The tumbrils toiling up the terrible way;
Even to-day your royal head may fall,
I think I will not hang myself to-day.

A Ballade of Theatricals (1912)

Though all the critics' canons grow--
Far seedier than the actors' own--
Although the cottage-door's too low--
Although the fairy's twenty stone--
Although, just like the telephone,
She comes by wire and not by wings,
Though all the mechanism's known--
Believe me, there are real things.

Yes, real people--even so--
Even in a theatre, truth is known,
Though the agnostic will not know,
And though the gnostic will not own,
There is a thing called skin and bone,
And many a man that struts and sings
Has been as stony-broke as stone . . .
Believe me, there are real things

There is an hour when all men go;
An hour when man is all alone.
When idle minstrels in a row
Went down with all the bugles blown--
When brass and hymn and drum went down,
Down in death's throat with thunderings--
Ah, though the unreal things have grown,
Believe me, there are real things.

ENVOY.

Prince, though your hair is not your own
And half your face held on by strings,
And if you sat, you'd smash your throne--
--Believe me, there are real things.

A Broad Minded Bishop Rebukes The Verminous St. Francis

"Even the religious poems are political, being a commentary on the current state of the Church of England"

If Brother Francis pardoned Brother Flea,
There still seems need of such strange charity,
Seeing he is, for all his gay goodwill,
Bitten by funny little creatures still.

By the Babe Unborn

If trees were tall and grasses short,
    As in some crazy tale,
If here and there a sea were blue
    Beyond the breaking pale,

If a fixed fire hung in the air
    To warm me one day through,
If deep green hair grew on great hills,
    I know what I should do.

In dark I lie; dreaming that there
    Are great eyes cold or kind,
And twisted streets and silent doors,
    And living men behind.

Let storm clouds come: better an hour,
    And leave to weep and fight,
Than all the ages I have ruled
    The empires of the night.

I think that if they gave me leave
    Within the world to stand,
I would be good through all the day
    I spent in fairyland.

They should not hear a word from me

Of selfishness or scorn,
If only I could find the door,
If only I were born.

A Child of the Snows

There is heard a hymn when the panes are dim,
  And never before or again,
When the nights are strong with a darkness long,
  And the dark is alive with rain.

Never we know but in sleet and in snow,
  The place where the great fires are,
That the midst of the earth is a raging mirth
  And the heart of the earth a star.

And at night we win to the ancient inn
  Where the child in the frost is furled,
We follow the feet where all souls meet
  At the inn at the end of the world.

The gods lie dead where the leaves lie red,
  For the flame of the sun is flown,
The gods lie cold where the leaves lie gold,
  And a Child comes forth alone.

The Convert

After one moment when I bowed my head
And the whole world turned over and came upright,
And I came out where the old road shone white,
I walked the ways and heard what all men said,
Forests of tongues, like autumn leaves unshed,
Being not unlovable but strange and light;
Old riddles and new creeds, not in despite
But softly, as men smile about the dead.

The sages have a hundred maps to give
That trace their crawling cosmos like a tree,
They rattle reason out through many a sieve
That stores the sand and lets the gold go free:
And all these things are less than dust to me
Because my name is Lazarus and I live.

The Deluge

Though giant rains put out the sun,
Here stand I for a sign.
Though earth be filled with waters dark,
My cup is filled with wine.
Tell to the trembling priests that here
Under the deluge rod,
One nameless, tattered, broken man
Stood up, and drank to God.

Sun has been where the rain is now,
Bees in the heat to hum,
Haply a humming maiden came,
Now let the deluge come:
Brown of aureole, green of garb,
Straight as a golden rod,
Drink to the throne of thunder now!
Drink to the wrath of God.

High in the wreck I held the cup,
I clutched my rusty sword,
I cocked my tattered feather
To the glory of the Lord.
Not undone were the heaven and earth,
This hollow world thrown up,
Before one man had stood up straight,
And drained it like a cup.

The Donkey

WHEN fishes flew and forests walked
And figs grew upon thorn,
Some moment when the moon was blood
Then surely I was born;

With monstrous head and sickening cry
And ears like errant wings,
The devil's walking parody
On all four-footed things.

The tattered outlaw of the earth,
Of ancient crooked will;
Starve, scourge, deride me: I am dumb,
I keep my secret still.

Fools! For I also had my hour;
One far fierce hour and sweet:
There was a shout about my ears,
And palms before my feet.

Elegy in a Country Churchyard

The men that worked for England
They have their graves at home:
And bees and birds of England
About the cross can roam.

But they that fought for England,
Following a falling star,
Alas, alas for England
They have their graves afar.

And they that rule in England,
In stately conclave met,
Alas, alas for England,
They have no graves as yet.

The Englishman

St George he was for England,
And before he killed the dragon
He drank a pint of English ale
Out of an English flagon.
For though he fast right readily
In hair-shirt or in mail,
It isn't safe to give him cakes
Unless you give him ale.
St George he was for England,
And right gallantly set free
The lady left for dragon's meat
And tied up to a tree;
But since he stood for England
And knew what England means,
Unless you give him bacon
You mustn't give him beans.
St George he is for England,
And shall wear the shield he wore
When we go out in armour
With battle-cross before.
But though he is jolly company
And very pleased to dine,
It isn't safe to give him nuts
Unless you give him wine.

Eternities

I cannot count the pebbles in the brook.
    Well hath He spoken: "Swear not by thy head.
    Thou knowest not the hairs," though He, we read,
Writes that wild number in His own strange book.

I cannot count the sands or search the seas,
    Death cometh, and I leave so much untrod.
    Grant my immortal aureole, O my God,
And I will name the leaves upon the trees,

In heaven I shall stand on gold and glass,
    Still brooding earth's arithmetic to spell;
    Or see the fading of the fires of hell
Ere I have thanked my God for all the grass.

Femina Contra Mundum

The sun was black with judgment, and the moon
    Blood: but between
I saw a man stand, saying: 'To me at least
    The grass is green.

'There was no star that I forgot to fear
    With love and wonder.
The birds have loved me'; but no answer came --
    Only the thunder.

Once more the man stood, saying: 'A cottage door,
    Wherethrough I gazed
That instant as I turned -- yea, I am vile;
    Yet my eyes blazed.

'For I had weighed the mountains in a balance,
    And the skies in a scale,
I come to sell the stars - old lamps for new -
    Old stars for sale.'

Then a calm voice fell all the thunder through,
    A tone less rough:
'Thou hast begun to love one of my works
    Almost enough.'

For a War Memorial

Suggested inscription probably not selected by the Committee.

The hucksters haggle in the mart
The cars and carts go by;
Senates and schools go droning on;
For dead things cannot die.

A storm stooped on the place of tombs
With bolts to blast and rive;
But these be names of many men
The lightning found alive.

If usurers rule and rights decay
And visions view once more
Great Carthage like a golden shell
Gape hollow on the shore,

Still to the last of crumbling time
Upon this stone be read
How many men of England died
To prove they were not dead.
Gold Leaves

Lo! I am come to autumn,
    When all the leaves are gold;

Grey hairs and golden leaves cry out
    The year and I are old.

In youth I sought the prince of men,
    Captain in cosmic wars,
Our Titan, even the weeds would show
    Defiant, to the stars.

But now a great thing in the street
    Seems any human nod,
Where shift in strange democracy
    The million masks of God.

In youth I sought the golden flower
    Hidden in wood or wold,
But I am come to autumn,
    When all the leaves are gold.

The Great Minimum

It is something to have wept as we have wept,
It is something to have done as we have done,
It is something to have watched when all men slept,
And seen the stars which never see the sun.

It is something to have smelt the mystic rose,
Although it break and leave the thorny rods,
It is something to have hungered once as those
Must hunger who have ate the bread of gods.

To have seen you and your unforgotten face,
Brave as a blast of trumpets for the fray,
Pure as white lilies in a watery space,
It were something, though you went from me today.

To have known the things that from the weak are furled,
Perilous ancient passions, strange and high;
It is something to be wiser than the world,
It is something to be older than the sky.

In a time of sceptic moths and cynic rusts,
And fattened lives that of their sweetness tire
In a world of flying loves and fading lusts,
It is something to be sure of a desire.

Lo, blessed are our ears for they have heard;

Yea, blessed are our eyes for they have seen:
Let the thunder break on man and beast and bird
And the lightning. It is something to have been.

The Higher Unity (1914)

The Rev. Isaiah Bunter has disappeared into the interior of the Solomon Islands, and it is feared that he may have been devoured by the natives, as there has been a considerable revival of religious customs among the Polynesians.-A real paragraph from a real newspaper; only the names altered.

It was Isaiah Bunter
Who sailed to the world's end,
And spread religion in a way
That he did not intend.

He gave, if not the gospel-feast,
At least a ritual meal;
And in a highly painful sense
He was devoured with zeal.

And who are we (as Henson says)
That we should close the door?
And should not Evangelicals
All jump at shedding Gore?

And many a man will melt in man,
Becoming one, not two,
When smacks across the startled earth
The Kiss of Kikuyu.

When Man is the Turk, and the Atheist,
Essene, Erastian[,] Whig,
And the Thug and the Druse and the Catholic
And the crew of the Captain's gig.

The Horrible History of Jones

Jones had a dog; it had a chain;
Not often worn, not causing pain;
But, as the I.K.L. had passed
Their 'Unleashed Cousins Act' at last,
Inspectors took the chain away;
Whereat the canine barked 'Hooray!'
At which, of course, the S.P.U.
(Whose Nervous Motorists' Bill was through)
Were forced to give the dog in charge
For being Audibly at Large.
None, you will say, were now annoyed,
Save, haply, Jones - the yard was void.
But something being in the lease
About 'alarms to aid the police,'
The U.S.U. annexed the yard
For having no sufficient guard.
Now if there's one condition
The C.C.P. are strong upon
It is that every house one buys
Must have a yard for exercise;
So Jones, as tenant, was unfit,
His state of health was proof of it.
Two doctors of the T.T.U.'s
Told him his legs, from long disuse,
Were atrophied; and saying 'So
From step to higher step we go

Till everything is New and True.'
They cut his legs off and withdrew.
You know the E.T.S.T.'s views
Are stronger than the T.T.U.'s:
And soon (as one may say) took wing
The Arms, though not the Man, I sing.
To see him sitting limbless there
Was more than the K.K. could bear.
'In mercy silence with all speed
That mouth there are no hands to feed;
What cruel sentimentalist,
O Jones, would doom thee to exist -
Clinging to selfish Selfhood yet?
Weak one! Such reasoning might upset
The Pump Act, and the accumulation
Of all constructive legislation;
Let us construct you up a bit - '
The head fell off when it was hit:
Then words did rise and honest doubt,
And four Commissioners sat about
Whether the slash that left him dead
Cut off his body or his head.

An author in the Isle of Wight
Observed with unconcealed delight
A land of just and old renown
Where Freedom slowly broadened down
From Precedent to Precedent.

And this, I think, was what he meant.

The House of Christmas

There fared a mother driven forth
Out of an inn to roam;
In the place where she was homeless
All men are at home.
The crazy stable close at hand,
With shaking timber and shifting sand,
Grew a stronger thing to abide and stand
Than the square stones of Rome.

For men are homesick in their homes,
And strangers under the sun,
And they lay on their heads in a foreign land
Whenever the day is done.
Here we have battle and blazing eyes,
And chance and honour and high surprise,
But our homes are under miraculous skies
Where the yule tale was begun.

A Child in a foul stable,
Where the beasts feed and foam;
Only where He was homeless
Are you and I at home;
We have hands that fashion and heads that know,
But our hearts we lost - how long ago!
In a place no chart nor ship can show

Under the sky's dome.

This world is wild as an old wives' tale,
And strange the plain things are,
The earth is enough and the air is enough
For our wonder and our war;
But our rest is as far as the fire-drake swings
And our peace is put in impossible things
Where clashed and thundered unthinkable wings
Round an incredible star.

To an open house in the evening
Home shall men come,
To an older place than Eden
And a taller town than Rome.
To the end of the way of the wandering star,
To the things that cannot be and that are,
To the place where God was homeless
And all men are at home.

The Human Tree

Many have Earth's lovers been,
Tried in seas and wars, I ween;
Yet the mightiest have I seen:
    Yea, the best saw I.
One that in a field alone
Stood up stiller than a stone
    Lest a moth should fly.

Birds had nested in his hair,
On his shoon were mosses rare,
Insect empires flourished there,
    Worms in ancient wars;
But his eyes burn like a glass,
Hearing a great sea of grass
    Roar towards the stars.

From them to the human tree
Rose a cry continually:
'Thou art still, our Father, we
    Fain would have thee nod.
Make the skies as blood below thee,
Though thou slay us, we shall know thee.
    Answer us, O God!

'Show thine ancient fame and thunder,
Split the stillness once asunder,

Lest we whisper, lest we wonder
    Art thou there at all?'
But I saw him there alone,
Standing stiller than a stone
    Lest a moth should fall.

A Hymn

O God of earth and altar,
Bow down and hear our cry,
Our earthly rulers falter,
Our people drift and die;
The walls of gold entomb us,
The swords of scorn divide,
Take not thy thunder from us,
But take away our pride.

From all that terror teaches,
From lies of tongue and pen,
From all the easy speeches
That comfort cruel men,
From sale and profanation
Of honour and the sword,
From sleep and from damnation,
Deliver us, good Lord.

Tie in a living tether
The prince and priest and thrall,
Bind all our lives together,
Smite us and save us all;
In ire and exultation
Aflame with faith, and free,
Lift up a living nation,
A single sword to thee.

The Judgment Of England

"Ill fares the land, to hastening ills a prey
Where Wealth accumulates and Men decay."
So rang of old the noble voice in vain
O'er the Last Peasants wandering on the plain,
Doom has reversed the riddle and the rhyme,
While sinks the commerce reared upon that crime,
The thriftless towns litter with lives undone,
To whom our madness left no joy but one;
And irony that glares like Judgment Day
Sees Men accumulate and Wealth decay.

The Last Hero

The wind blew out from Bergen from the dawning to the day,
There was a wreck of trees and fall of towers a score of miles away,
And drifted like a livid leaf I go before its tide,
Spewed out of house and stable, beggared of flag and bride.
The heavens are bowed about my head, shouting like seraph wars,
With rains that might put out the sun and clean the sky of stars,
Rains like the fall of ruined seas from secret worlds above,
The roaring of the rains of God none but the lonely love.
Feast in my hall, O foemen, and eat and drink and drain,
You never loved the sun in heaven as I have loved the rain.

The chance of battle changes -- so may all battle be;
I stole my lady bride from them, they stole her back from me.
I rent her from her red-roofed hall, I rode and saw arise,
More lovely than the living flowers the hatred in her eyes.
She never loved me, never bent, never was less divine;
The sunset never loved me, the wind was never mine.
Was it all nothing that she stood imperial in duresse?

Silence itself made softer with the sweeping of her dress.
O you who drain the cup of life, O you who wear the crown,
You never loved a woman's smile as I have loved her frown.

The wind blew out from Bergen to the dawning of the day,
They ride and run with fifty spears to break and bar my way,
I shall not die alone, alone, but kin to all the powers,
As merry as the ancient sun and fighting like the flowers.
How white their steel, how bright their eyes! I love each laughing knave,
Cry high and bid him welcome to the banquet of the brave.
Yea, I will bless them as they bend and love them where they lie,
When on their skulls the sword I swing falls shattering from the sky.
The hour when death is like a light and blood is like a rose,-
You never loved your friends, my friends, as I shall love my foes.

Know you what earth shall lose to-night, what rich uncounted loans,
What heavy gold of tales untold you bury with my bones?

My loves in deep dim meadows, my ships that rode at ease,
Ruffling the purple plumage of strange and secret seas.
To see this fair earth as it is to me alone was given,
The blow that breaks my brow to-night shall break the dome of heaven.
The skies I saw, the trees I saw after no eyes shall see,
To-night I die the death of God; the stars shall die with me;
One sound shall sunder all the spears and break the trumpet's breath:
You never laughed in all your life as I shall laugh in death.

A Little Litany

When God turned back eternity and was young,
Ancient of Days, grown little for your mirth
(As under the low arch the land is bright)
Peered through you, gate of heaven--and saw the earth.

Or shutting out his shining skies awhile
Built you about him for a house of gold
To see in pictured walls his storied world
Return upon him as a tale is told.

Or found his mirror there; the only glass
That would not break with that unbearable light
Till in a corner of the high dark house
God looked on God, as ghosts meet in the night.

Star of his morning; that unfallen star
In that strange starry overturn of space
When earth and sky changed places for an hour
And heaven looked upwards in a human face.

Or young on your strong knees and lifted up
Wisdom cried out, whose voice is in the street,
And more than twilight of twiformed cherubim
Made of his throne indeed a mercy-seat.

Or risen from play at your pale raiment's hem
God, grown adventurous from all time's repose,
Or your tall body climed the ivory tower
And kissed upon your mouth the mystic rose.

The Logical Vegetarian (1915)

You will find me drinking rum,
    Like a sailor in a slum,
You will find me drinking beer like a Bavarian.
    You will find me drinking gin
    In the lowest kind of inn,
Because I am a rigid Vegetarian.

    So I cleared the inn of wine,
    And I tried to climb the sign,
And I tried to hail the constable as "Marion."
    But he said I couldn't speak,
    And he bowled me to the Beak
Because I was a Happy Vegetarian.

    Oh, I knew a Doctor Gluck,
    And his nose it had a hook,
And his attitudes were anything but Aryan;
    So I gave him all the pork
That I had, upon a fork;
Because I am myself a Vegetarian.

I am silent in the Club,
I am silent in the pub,
I am silent on a bally peak in Darien;
For I stuff away for life
Shoving peas in with a knife,
Because I am at heart a Vegetarian.

No more the milk of cows
Shall pollute my private house
Than the milk of the wild mares of the Barbarian;
I will stick to port and sherry,
For they are so very, very
So very, very, very Vegetarian.

The Mystery

If sunset clouds could grow on trees
It would but match the may in flower;
And skies be underneath the seas
No topsyturvier than a shower.

If mountains rose on wings to wander
They were no wilder than a cloud;
Yet all my praise is mean as slander,
Mean as these mean words spoken aloud.

And never more than now I know
That man's first heaven is far behind;
Unless the blazing seraph's blow
Has left him in the garden blind.

Witness, O Sun that blinds our eyes,
Unthinkable and unthankable King,
That though all other wonder dies
I wonder at not wondering.

The Myth of Arthur

O learned man who never learned to learn,
Save to deduce, by timid steps and small,
From towering smoke that fire can never burn
And from tall tales that men were never tall.
Say, have you thought what manner of man it is
Of who men say "He could strike giants down"?
Or what strong memories over time's abyss
Bore up the pomp of Camelot and the crown.
And why one banner all the background fills,
Beyond the pageants of so many spears,
And by what witchery in the western hills
A throne stands empty for a thousand years.
Who hold, unheeding this immense impact,
Immortal story for a mortal sin;
Lest human fable touch historic fact,
Chase myths like moths, and fight them with a pin.
Take comfort; rest--there needs not this ado.
You shall not be a myth, I promise you.

The New Fiction

Little Blue-Fits has lost his wits,
And doesn't know where to find them;
Leave them alone and they'll come home,
And leave their tales behind them.

The remarkable tales, with remarkable sales,
And Bonnets and Bees in disorder;
For the Bonnets we view are exceedingly Blue,
And decidedly over the Border.

The New Omar

A Book of verses underneath the bough,
    Provided that the verses do not scan,
A loaf of bread, a jug of wine and Thou,
    Short-haired, all angles, looking like a man.

But let the wine be unfermented, Pale,
    Of chemicals compounded, God knows how-
This were indeed the Prophet's Paradise,
    O Paradise were Wilderness enow.

The Old Song

A livid sky on London
And like the iron steeds that rear
A shock of engines halted
And I knew the end was near:
And something said that far away, over the hills and far away
There came a crawling thunder and the end of all things here.
For London Bridge is broken down, broken down, broken down,
As digging lets the daylight on the suken streets of yore,
The lightning looked on London town, the broken bridge of London town.
The ending of a broken road where men shall go no more.

I saw the kings of London town,
The kings that buy and sell,
That built it up with penny loaves
And penny lies as well:

And where the streets were paved with gold the shrivelled paper shone for gold,
The scorching light of promises that pave the streets of hell.
For penny loaves will melt away, melt away, melt away,
Mock the men that haggled in the grain they did not

grow;
With hungry faces in the gate, a hundred thousand in the gate,
A thunder-flash on London and the finding of the foe.

I heard the hundred pin-makers
Slow down their racking din,
Till in the stillness men could hear
The dropping of the pin:
And somewhere men without the wall, beneath the wood, without the wall,
Had found the place where London ends and England can begin.
For pins and needles bend and break, bend and break, bend and break,
Faster than the breaking spears or the bending of the bow,
Of pagents pale in thunder-light, 'twixt thunderload and thunderlight,
The Hundreds marching on the hills in the wars of long ago.

I saw great Cobbett riding,
The horseman of the shires;
And his face was red with judgement
And a light of Luddite fires:
And south to Sussex and the sea the lights leapt up for liberty,

The trumpet of the yeomanry, the hammer of the squires;
For bars of iron rust away, rust away, rust away,
Rend before the hammer and the horseman riding in,
Crying that all men at the last, and at the worst and at the last,
Have found the place where England ends and England can begin.

His horse-hoofs go before you
Far beyond your bursting tyres;
And time is bridged behind him
And our sons are with our sires.

A trailing meteor on the Downs he rides above the rotting towns,
The Horseman of Apocalypse, the Rider of the Shires.
For London Bridge is broken down, broken down, broken down;
Blow the horn of Huntington from Scotland to the sea -
...Only flash of thunder-light, a flying dream of thunder-light,
Had shown under the shattered sky a people that were free.

On the Disastrous Spread of Aestheticism in all Classes

Impetuously I sprang from bed,
Long before lunch was up,
That I might drain the dizzy dew
From the day's first golden cup.

In swift devouring ecstasy
Each toil in turn was done;
I had done lying on the lawn
Three minutes after one.

For me, as Mr. Wordsworth says,
The duties shine like stars;
I formed my uncle's character,
Decreasing his cigars.

But could my kind engross me? No!
Stern Art-what sons escape her?
Soon I was drawing Gladstone's nose
On scraps of blotting paper.

Then on-to play one-fingered tunes
Upon my aunt's piano.
In short, I have a headlong soul,
I much resemble Hanno.

(Forgive the entrance of the not
    Too cogent Carthaginian.
It may have been to make a rhyme;
    I lean to that opinion.)

Then my great work of book research
    Till dusk I took in hand-
The forming of a final, sound
    Opinion on The Strand.

But when I quenched the midnight oil,
    And closed the Referee,
Whose thirty volumes folio
    I take to bed with me,

I had a rather funny dream,
    Intense, that is, and mystic;
I dreamed that, with one leap and yell,
    The world became artistic.

The Shopmen, when their souls were still,
    Declined to open shops-
And Cooks recorded frames of mind
    In sad and subtle chops.

The stars were weary of routine:
    The trees in the plantation
Were growing every fruit at once,

In search of sensation.

The moon went for a moonlight stroll,
And tried to be a bard,
And gazed enraptured at itself:
I left it trying hard.

The sea had nothing but a mood
Of 'vague ironic gloom,'
With which t'explain its presence in
My upstairs drawing-room.

The sun had read a little book
That struck him with a notion:
He drowned himself and all his fires
Deep in a hissing ocean.

Then all was dark, lawless, and lost:
I heard great devilish wings:
I knew that Art had won, and snapt
The Covenant of Things.

I cried aloud, and I awoke,
New labours in my head.
I set my teeth, and manfully
Began to lie in bed.

Toiling, rejoicing, sorrowing,

So I my life conduct.
Each morning see some task begun,
Each evening see it chucked.

But still, in sudden moods of dusk,
I hear those great weird wings,
Feel vaguely thankful to the vast
Stupidity of things.

Envoi

Clear was the night: the moon was young
The larkspurs in the plots
Mingled their orange with the gold
Of the forget-me-nots.

The poppies seemed a silver mist:
So darkly fell the gloom.
You scarce had guessed yon crimson streaks
Were buttercups in bloom.

But one thing moved: a little child
Crashed through the flower and fern:
And all my soul rose up to greet
The sage of whom I learn.

I looked into his awful eyes:
I waited his decree:

I made ingenious attempts
    To sit upon his knee.

The babe upraised his wondering eyes,
    And timidly he said,
"A trend towards experiment
    In modern minds is bred.

"I feel the will to roam, to learn
    By test, experience, nous,
That fire is hot and ocean deep,
    And wolves carnivorous.

"My brain demands complexity,"
    The lisping cherub cried.
I looked at him, and only said,
    "Go on. The world is wide."

A tear rolled down his pinafore,
    "Yet from my life must pass
The simple love of sun and moon,
    The old games in the grass;

"Now that my back is to my home
    Could these again be found?"
I looked on him and only said,
    "Go on. The world is round."

The Philanthropist

Abou Ben Adhem (may his tribe decrease
By cautious birth-control and die in peace)
Mellow with learning lightly took the word
That marked him not with them that love the Lord,
And told the angel of the book and pen
"Write me as one that loves his fellow-men:
For them alone I labour; to reclaim
The ragged roaming Bedouin and to tame
To ordered service; to uproot their vine
Who mock the Prophet, being mad with wine,
Let daylight through their tents and through their lives,
Number their camels, even count their wives;
Plot out the desert into streets and squares,
And count it a more fruitful work than theirs
Who lift a vain and visionary love
To your vague Allah in the skies above."

Gently replied the angel of the pen:
"Labour in peace and love your fellow-men:
And love not God, since men alone are dear,
Only fear God; for you have Cause to fear."

The Praise of Dust

"What of vile dust?" the preacher said.
Methought the whole world woke,
The dead stone lived beneath my foot,
And my whole body spoke.

"You, that play tyrant to the dust,
And stamp its wrinkled face,
This patient star that flings you not
Far into homeless space.

"Come down out of your dusty shrine
The living dust to see,
The flowers that at your sermon's end
Stand blazing silently.

"Rich white and blood-red blossom; stones,
Lichens like fire encrust;
A gleam of blue, a glare of gold,
The vision of the dust.

"Pass them all by: till, as you come
Where, at a city's edge,
Under a tree--I know it well--
Under a lattice ledge,

"The sunshine falls on one brown head.
    You, too, O cold of clay,
Eater of stones, may haply hear
    The trumpets of that day

"When God to all his paladins
    By his own splendour swore
To make a fairer face than heaven,
    Of dust and nothing more."

A Prayer in Darkness

This much, O heaven-if I should brood or rave,
Pity me not; but let the world be fed,
Yea, in my madness if I strike me dead,
Heed you the grass that grows upon my grave.

If I dare snarl between this sun and sod,
Whimper and clamour, give me grace to own,
In sun and rain and fruit in season shown,
The shining silence of the scorn of God.

Thank God the stars are set beyond my power,
If I must travail in a night of wrath,
Thank God my tears will never vex a moth,
Nor any curse of mine cut down a flower.

Men say the sun was darkened: yet I had
Thought it beat brightly, even on-Calvary:
And He that hung upon the Torturing Tree
Heard all the crickets singing, and was glad.

The Rolling English Road (1914)

Before the Roman came to Rye or out to Severn strode,
The rolling English drunkard made the rolling English road,
A reeling road, a rolling road, that rambles round the shire,
And after him the parson ran, the sexton and the squire,
A merry road, a mazy road, and such as we did tread,
The night we went to Birmingham by way of Beachy Head.

I knew no harm of Bonaparte and plenty of the Squire,
And for to fight the Frenchman I did not much desire;
But I did bash their baggonets because they came arrayed
To straighten out the crooked road an English drunkard made,
Where you and I went down the lane with ale-mugs in our hands,
The night we went to Glastonbury by way of Goodwin Sands.

His sins they were forgiven him; or why do flowers run
Behind him; and the hedges all strengthening in the sun?
The wild thing went from left to right and knew not which was which,
But the wild rose was above him when they found him in the ditch.

God pardon us, nor harden us; we did not see so clear
The night we went to Bannockburn by way of Brighton Pier.

My friends, we will not go again or ape an ancient rage,
Or stretch the folly of our youth to be the shame of age,
But walk with clearer eyes and ears this path that wandereth,
And see undrugged in evening light the decent inn of death;
For there is good news yet to hear and fine things to be seen,
Before we go to Paradise by way of Kensal Green.

The Secret People

Smile at us, pay us, pass us; but do not quite forget;
For we are the people of England, that never have spoken yet.
There is many a fat farmer that drinks less cheerfully,
There is many a free French peasant who is richer and sadder than we.
There are no folk in the whole world so helpless or so wise.
There is hunger in our bellies, there is laughter in our eyes;
You laugh at us and love us, both mugs and eyes are wet:
Only you do not know us. For we have not spoken yet.

The fine French kings came over in a flutter of flags and dames.
We liked their smiles and battles, but we never could say their names.
The blood ran red to Bosworth and the high French lords went down;
There was naught but a naked people under a naked crown.
And the eyes of the King's Servants turned terribly every way,
And the gold of the King's Servants rose higher every day.
They burnt the homes of the shaven men, that had been

quaint and kind,
Till there was no bed in a monk's house, nor food that man could find.
The inns of God where no man paid, that were the wall of the weak.
The King's Servants ate them all. And still we did not speak.

And the face of the King's Servants grew greater than the King:
He tricked them, and they trapped him, and stood round him in a ring.
The new grave lords closed round him, that had eaten the abbey's fruits,
And the men of the new religion, with their bibles in their boots,
We saw their shoulders moving, to menace or discuss,
And some were pure and some were vile; but none took heed of us.
We saw the King as they killed him, and his face was proud and pale;
And a few men talked of freedom, while England talked of ale.

A war that we understood not came over the world and woke
Americans, Frenchmen, Irish; but we knew not the things they spoke.

They talked about rights and nature and peace and the people's reign:
And the squires, our masters, bade us fight; and scorned us never again.
Weak if we be for ever, could none condemn us then;
Men called us serfs and drudges; men knew that we were men.
In foam and flame at Trafalgar, on Albuera plains,
We did and died like lions, to keep ourselves in chains,
We lay in living ruins; firing and fearing not
The strange fierce face of the Frenchmen who knew for what they fought,
And the man who seemed to be more than a man we strained against and broke;
And we broke our own rights with him. And still we never spoke.

Our patch of glory ended; we never heard guns again.
But the squire seemed struck in the saddle; he was foolish, as if in pain,
He leaned on a staggering lawyer, he clutched a cringing Jew,
He was stricken; it may be, after all, he was stricken at Waterloo.
Or perhaps the shades of the shaven men, whose spoil is in his house,
Come back in shining shapes at last to spoil his last carouse:

We only know the last sad squires rode slowly towards the sea,
And a new people takes the land: and still it is not we.

They have given us into the hand of new unhappy lords,
Lords without anger or honour, who dare not carry their swords.
They fight by shuffling papers; they have bright dead alien eyes;
They look at our labour and laughter as a tired man looks at flies.
And the load of their loveless pity is worse than the ancient wrongs,
Their doors are shut in the evening; and they know no songs.

We hear men speaking for us of new laws strong and sweet,
Yet is there no man speaketh as we speak in the street.
It may be we shall rise the last as Frenchmen rose the first,
Our wrath come after Russia's wrath and our wrath be the worst.
It may be we are meant to mark with our riot and our rest
God's scorn for all men governing. It may be beer is best.
But we are the people of England; and we have not spoken yet.
Smile at us, pay us, pass us. But do not quite forget.

The Skeleton

Chattering finch and water-fly
Are not merrier than I;
Here among the flowers I lie
Laughing everlastingly.
No; I may not tell the best;
Surely, friends, I might have guessed
Death was but the good King's jest,
It was hid so carefully.

The Song Against Grocers

God made the wicked Grocer
For a mystery and a sign,
That men might shun the awful shops
And go to inns to dine;
Where the bacon's on the rafter
And the wine is in the wood,
And God that made good laughter
Has seen that they are good.

The evil-hearted Grocer
Would call his mother "Ma'am,"
And bow at her and bob at her,
Her aged soul to damn,
And rub his horrid hands and ask
What article was next
Though MORTIS IN ARTICULO
Should be her proper text.

His props are not his children,
But pert lads underpaid,
Who call out "Cash!" and bang about
To work his wicked trade;
He keeps a lady in a cage
Most cruelly all day,
And makes her count and calls her "Miss"
Until she fades away.

The righteous minds of innkeepers
Induce them now and then
To crack a bottle with a friend
Or treat unmoneyed men,
But who hath seen the Grocer
Treat housemaids to his teas
Or crack a bottle of fish sauce
Or stand a man a cheese?

He sells us sands of Araby
As sugar for cash down;
He sweeps his shop and sells the dust
The purest salt in town,
He crams with cans of poisoned meat
Poor subjects of the King,
And when they die by thousands
Why, he laughs like anything.

The wicked Grocer groces
In spirits and in wine,
Not frankly and in fellowship
As men in inns do dine;
But packed with soap and sardines
And carried off by grooms,
For to be snatched by Duchesses
And drunk in dressing-rooms.

The hell-instructed Grocer
Has a temple made of tin,
And the ruin of good innkeepers
Is loudly urged therein;
But now the sands are running out
From sugar of a sort,
The Grocer trembles; for his time,
Just like his weight, is short.

The Song of the Oak

The Druids waved their golden knives
And danced around the Oak
When they had sacrificed a man;
But though the learned search and scan
No single modern person can
Entirely see the joke.
But though they cut the throats of men
They cut not down the tree,
And from the blood the saplings spring
Of oak-woods yet to be.
    But Ivywood, Lord Ivywood,
    He rots the tree as ivy would,
    He clings and crawls as ivy would
    About the sacred tree.

King Charles he fled from Worcester fight
And hid him in the Oak;
In convent schools no man of tact
Would trace and praise his every act,
Or argue that he was in fact
A strict and sainted bloke.
But not by him the sacred woods
Have lost their fancies free,
And though he was extremely big
He did not break the tree.
    But Ivywood, Lord Ivywood,

He breaks the tree as ivy would,
And eats the woods as ivy would
Between us and the sea.

Great Collingwood walked down the glade
And flung the acorns free,
That oaks might still be in the grove
As oaken as the beams above,
When the great Lover sailors love
Was kissed by Death at aea.
But though for him the oak-trees fell
To build the oaken ships,
The woodman worshipped what he smote
And honoured even the chips.
But Ivywood, Lord Ivywood,
He hates the tree as ivy would,
As the dragon of the ivy would
That has us in his grips.

The Song of Right and Wrong

Feast on wine or fast on water
And your honour shall stand sure,
God Almighty's son and daughter
He the valiant, she the pure;
If an angel out of heaven
Brings you other things to drink,
Thank him for his kind attentions,
Go and pour them down the sink.

Tea is like the East he grows in,
A great yellow Mandarin
With urbanity of manner
And unconsciousness of sin;
All the women, like a harem,
At his pig-tail troop along;
And, like all the East he grows in,
He is Poison when he's strong.

Tea, although an Oriental,
Is a gentleman at least;
Cocoa is a cad and coward,
Cocoa is a vulgar beast,
Cocoa is a dull, disloyal,
Lying, crawling cad and clown,
And may very well be grateful
To the fool that takes him down.

As for all the windy waters,
They were rained like tempests down
When good drink had been dishonoured
By the tipplers of the town;
When red wine had brought red ruin
And the death-dance of our times,
Heaven sent us Soda Water
As a torment for our crimes.

The Song of the Strange Ascetic (1913)

If I had been a heathen,
I'd have praised the purple vine,
My slaves should dig the vineyards,
And I would drink the wine;
But Higgins is a heathen,
And his slaves grow lean and grey,
That he may drink some tepid milk
Exactly twice a day.

If I had been a heathen,
I'd have crowned Neaera's curls,
And filled my life with love affairs,
My house with dancing girls;
But Higgins is a heathen,
And to lecture rooms is forced,
Where his aunts, who are not married,
Demand to be divorced.

If I had been a heathen,
I'd have sent my armies forth,
And dragged behind my chariots
The Chieftains of the North;
But Higgins is a heathen,
And he drives the dreary quill,
To lend the poor that funny cash
That makes them poorer still.

If I had been a heathen,
I'd have piled my pyre on high,
And in a great red whirlwind
Gone roaring to the sky;
But Higgins is a heathen,
And a richer man than I:
And they put him in an oven,
Just as if he were a pie.

Now who that runs can read it,
The riddle that I write,
Of why this poor old sinner
Should sin without delight;
But I, I cannot read it
(Although I run and run),
Of them that do not have the faith,
And will not have the fun.
The Song of Quoodle

They haven't got no noses,
The fallen sons of Eve;
Even the smell of roses
Is not what they supposes;
But more than mind discloses
And more than men believe.

They haven't got no noses,

They cannot even tell
When door and darkness closes
The park a Jew encloses,
Where even the law of Moses
Will let you steal a smell.

The brilliant smell of water,
The brave smell of a stone,
The smell of dew and thunder,
The old bones buried under,
Are things in which they blunder
And err, if left alone.

The wind from winter forests,
The scent of scentless flowers,
The breath of brides' adorning,
The smell of snare and warning,
The smell of Sunday morning,
God gave to us for ours

* *

And Quoodle here discloses
All things that Quoodle can,
They haven't got no noses,
They haven't got no noses,
And goodness only knowses
The Noselessness of Man.

The Song Of The Wheels

King Dives he was walking in his garden all alone,
Where his flowers are made of iron and his trees are made of stone,
And his hives are full of thunder and the lightning leaps and kills,
For the mills of God grind slowly; and he works with other mills.
Dives found a mighty silence; and he missed the throb and leap,
The noise of all the sleepless creatures singing him to sleep.
And he said: "A screw has fallen-or a bolt has slipped aside-
Some little thing has shifted": and the little things replied:

"Call upon the wheels, master, call upon the wheels;
We are taking rest, master, finding how it feels,
Strict the law of thine and mine: theft we ever shun-
All the wheels are thine, master-tell the wheels to run!
Yea, the Wheels are mighty gods-set them going then!
We are only men, master, have you heard of men?

"O, they live on earth like fishes, and a gasp is all their breath.
God for empty honours only gave them death and scorn

of death,
And you walk the worms for carpet and you tread a stone that squeals
Only, God that made them worms did not make them wheels.
Man shall shut his heart against you and you shall not find the spring.
Man who wills the thing he wants not, the intolerable thing-
Once he likes his empty belly better than your empty head
Earth and heaven are dumb before him: he is stronger than the dead.

"Call upon the wheels, master, call upon the wheels,
Steel is beneath your hand, stone beneath your heels,
Steel will never laugh aloud, hearing what we heard,
Stone will never break its heart, mad with hope deferred-
Men of tact that arbitrate, slow reform that heals-
Save the stinking grease, master, save it for the wheels.

"King Dives in the garden, we have naught to give or hold-
(Even while the baby came alive the rotten sticks were sold.)
The savage knows a cavern and the peasants keep a plot,
Of all the things that men have had-lo! we have them not.

Not a scrap of earth where ants could lay their eggs-
Only this poor lump of earth that walks about on legs-
Only this poor wandering mansion, only these two walking trees,
Only hands and hearts and stomachs-what have you to do with these?
You have engines big and burnished, tall beyond our fathers' ken,
Why should you make peace and traffic with such feeble folk as men?

"Call upon the wheels, master, call upon the wheels,
They are deaf to demagogues, deaf to crude appeals;
Are our hands our own, master?-how the doctors doubt!
Are our legs our own, master? wheels can run without-
Prove the points are delicate-they will understand.
All the wheels are loyal; see how still they stand!"

King Dives he was walking in his garden in the sun,
He shook his hand at heaven, and he called the wheels to run,
And the eyes of him were hateful eyes, the lips of him were curled,
And he called upon his father that is lord below the world,
Sitting in the Gate of Treason, in the gate of broken seals,
"Bend and bind them, bend and bind them, bend and bind them into wheels,

Then once more in all my garden there may swing and sound and sweep-

The noise of all the sleepless things that sing the soul to sleep."

Call upon the wheels, master, call upon the wheels,
Weary grow the holidays when you miss the meals,
Through the Gate of Treason, through the gate within,
Cometh fear and greed of fame, cometh deadly sin;
If a man grow faint, master, take him ere he kneels,
Take him, break him, rend him, end him, roll him, crush him with the wheels.

Songs of Education

History

The Roman threw us a road, a road,
And sighed and strolled away:
The Saxon gave us a raid, a raid,
A raid that came to stay;
The Dane went west, but the Dane confessed
That he went a bit too far;
And we all became, by another name,
The Imperial race we are.

The Imperial race, the inscrutable race,
The invincible race we are.

Though Sussex hills are bare, are bare,
And Sussex weald is wide,
From Chichester to Chester
Men saw the Norman ride;
He threw his sword in the air and sang
To a sort of a light guitar;
It was all the same, for we all became
The identical nobs we are.

The identical nobs, individual nobs,
Unmistakable nobs we are.

The people lived on the land, the land,
They pottered about and prayed;

They built a cathedral here and there
Or went on a small crusade:
Till the bones of Becket were bundled out
For the fun of a fat White Czar,
And we all became, in spoil and flame,
The intelligent lot we are.

The intelligent lot, the intuitive lot,
The infallible lot we are.

O Warwick woods are green, are green,
But Warwick trees can fall:
And Birmingham grew so big, so big,
And Stratford stayed so small.
Till the hooter howled to the morning lark
That sang to the morning star:
And we all became, in freedom's name,
The fortunate chaps we are.

The fortunate chaps, felicitous chaps,
The fairy-like chaps we are.

The people, they left the land, the land,
But they went on working hard:
And the village green that had got mislaid
Turned up in the squire's back-yard:
But twenty men of us all got work
On a bit of his motor car;

And we all became, with the world's acclaim,
The marvellous mugs we are:

The marvellous mugs, miraculous mugs,
The mystical mugs we are.
Geography
The earth is a place on which England is found,
And you find it however you twirl the globe round;
For the spots are all red and the rest is all grey,
And that is the meaning of Empire Day.

Gibraltar's a rock that you see very plain,
And attached to its base is the district of Spain.
And the island of Malta is marked further on,
Where some natives were known as the Knights of St. John.

Then Cyprus, and east to the Suez Canal,
That was conquered by Dizzy and Rothschild his pal
With the Sword of the Lord in the old English way:
And that is the meaning of Empire Day.

Our principal imports come far as Cape Horn;
For necessities, cocoa; for luxuries, corn;
Thus Brahmins are born for the rice-field, and thus,
The Gods made the Greeks to grow currants for us;
Of earth's other tributes are plenty to choose,
Tobacco and petrol and Jazzing and Jews:

The Jazzing will pass but the Jews they will stay;
And that is the meaning of Empire Day.

Our principle exports, all labelled and packed,
At the ends of the earth are delivered intact:
Our soap or our salmon can travel in tins
Between the two poles and as like as two pins;
So that Lancashire merchants whenever they like
Can water the beer of a man in Klondike
Or poison the meat of a man in Bombay;
And that is the meaning of Empire Day.

The day of St. George is a musty affair
Which Russians and Greeks are permitted to share;
The day of Trafalgar is Spanish in name
And the Spaniards refuse to pronounce it the same;
But the day of the Empire from Canada came
With Morden and Borden and Beaverbrook's fame
And saintly seraphical souls such as they:
And that is the meaning of Empire Day.
The Higher Mathematics
Twice one is two,
Twice two is four,
But twice two is ninety-six if you know the way to score.
Half of two is one,
Half of four is two,
But half of four is forty per cent. if your name is Montagu:
For everything else is on the square

If done by the best quadratics;
And nothing is low in High Finance
Or the Higher Mathematics.

A straight line is straight
And a square mile is flat:
But you learn in trigonometrics a trick worth two of that.
Two straight lines
Can't enclose a Space,
But they can enclose a Corner to support the Chosen Race:
For you never know what Dynamics do
With the lower truths of Statics;
And half of two is a touring car
In the Higher Mathematics.

There is a place apart
Beyond the solar ray,
Where parallel straight lines can meet in an unofficial way.
There is a room that holds
The examiner or his clerks,
Where you can square the circle or the man that gives the marks.
Where you hide in the cellar and then look down
On the poets that live in the attics;
For the whole of the house is upside down
In the Higher Mathematics.

St. Francis Xavier

He left his dust, by all the myriad tread
Of yon dense millions trampled to the strand,
Or 'neath some cross forgotten lays his head
Where dark seas whiten on a lonely land:
He left his work, what all his life had planned,
A waning flame to flicker and to fall,
Mid the huge myths his toil could scarce withstand,
And the light died in temple and in hall,
And the old twilight sank and settled over all.

He left his name, a murmur in the East,
That dies to silence amid older creeds,
With which he strove in vain: the fiery priest
Of faiths less fitted to their ruder needs:
As some lone pilgrim, with his staff and beads,
Mid forest-brutes whom ignorance makes tame,
He dwelt, and sowed an Eastern Church's seeds
He reigned, a teacher and a priest of fame:
He died and dying left a murmur and a name.

He died: and she, the Church that bade him go,
Yon dim Enchantress with her mystic claim,
Has ringed his forehead with her aureole-glow,
And monkish myths, and all the whispered fame
Of miracle, has clung about his name:
So Rome has said: but we, what answer we

Who in grim Indian gods and rites of shame
O'er all the East the teacher's failure see,
His Eastern Church a dream, his toil a vanity.

This then we say: as Time's dark face at last
Moveth its lips of thunder to decree
The doom that grew through all the murmuring past
To be the canon of the times to be:
No child of truth or priest of progress he,
Yet not the less a hero of his wars
Striving to quench the light he could not see,
And God, who knoweth all that makes and mars,
Judges his soul unseen which throbs among the stars.

God only knows, man failing in his choice,
How far apparent failure may succeed,
God only knows what echo of His voice
Lives in the cant of many a fallen creed,
God only gives the labourer his meed
For all the lingering influence widely spread,
Broad branching into many a word and deed
When dim oblivion veils the fountain-head;
So lives and lingers on the spirit of the dead.

This then we say: let all things further rest
And this brave life, with many thousands more,
Be gathered up in the eternal's breast
In that dim past his Love is bending o'er:

Healing all shattered hopes and failure sore:
Since he had bravely looked on death and pain
For what he chose to worship and adore,
Cast boldly down his life for loss or gain
In the eternal lottery: not to be in vain.

The Strange Music

Other loves may sink and settle, other loves may loose and slack,
But I wander like a minstrel with a harp upon my back,
Though the harp be on my bosom, though I finger and I fret,
Still, my hope is all before me; for I cannot play it yet.

In your strings is hid a music that no hand hath e'er let fall,
In your soul is sealed a pleasure that you have not known at all;
Pleasure subtle as your spirit, strange and slender as your frame,
Fiercer than the pain that folds you, softer than your sorrow's name.

Not as mine, my soul's annointed, not as mine the rude and light
Easy mirth of many faces, swaggering pride of song and fight;
Something stranger, something sweeter, something waiting you afar,
Secret as your stricken senses, magic as your sorrows are.

But on this, God's harp supernal, stretched but to be stricken once,
Hoary time is a beginner, Life a bungler, Death a dunce.
But I will not fear to match them - no by God, I will not fear,
I will learn you, I will play you and the stars stand still to hear.

The Sword of Suprise

Sunder me from my bones, O sword of God
Till they stand stark and strange as do the trees;
That I whose heart goes up with the soaring woods
May marvel as much at these.

Sunder me from my blood that in the dark
I hear that red ancestral river run
Like branching buried floods that find the sea
But never see the sun.

Give me miraculous eyes to see my eyes
Those rolling mirrors made alive in me
Terrible crystals more incredible
Than all the things they see

Sunder me from my soul, that I may see
The sins like streaming wounds, the life's brave beat
Till I shall save myself as I would save
A stranger in the street.

To Belloc

For every tiny town or place
God made the stars especially;
Babies look up with owlish face
And see them tangled in a tree;
You saw a moon from Sussex Downs,
A Sussex moon, untravelled still,
I saw a moon that was the town's,
The largest lamp on Campden Hill.

Yea; Heaven is everywhere at home
The big blue cap that always fits,
And so it is (be calm; they come
To goal at last, my wandering wits),
So is it with the heroic thing;
This shall not end for the world's end
And though the sullen engines swing,
Be you not much afraid, my friend.

This did not end by Nelson's urn
Where an immortal England sits--
Nor where your tall young men in turn
Drank death like wine at Austerlitz.
And when the pedants bade us mark
What cold mechanic happenings
Must come; our souls said in the dark,
"Belike; but there are likelier things."

Likelier across these flats afar
These sulky levels smooth and free
The drums shall crash a waltz of war
And Death shall dance with Liberty;
Likelier the barricades shall blare
Slaughter below and smoke above,
And death and hate and hell declare
That men have found a thing to love.

Far from your sunny uplands set
I saw the dream; the streets I trod
The lit straight streets shot out and met
The starry streets that point to God.
This legend of an epic hour
A child I dreamed, and dream it still,
Under the great grey water-tower
That strikes the stars on Campden Hill

To St. Michael in Time of Peace

Michael, Michael: Michael of the Morning,
Michael of the Army of the Lord,
Stiffen thou the hand upon the still sword, Michael,
Folded and shut upon the sheathed sword, Michael,
Under the fullness of the white robes falling,
Gird us with the secret of the sword.

When the world cracked because of a sneer in heaven,
Leaving out for all time a scar upon the sky,
Thou didst rise up against the Horror in the highest,
Dragging down the highest that looked down on the Most High:
Rending from the seventh heaven the hell of exaltation
Down the seven heavens till the dark seas burn:
Thou that in thunder threwest down the Dragon
Knowest in what silence the Serpent can return.

Down through the universe the vast night falling
(Michael, Michael: Michael of the Morning!)
Far down the universe the deep calms calling
(Michael, Michael: Michael of the Sword!)
Bid us not forget in the baths of all forgetfulness,
In the sigh long drawn from the frenzy and the fretfulness
In the huge holy sempiternal silence
In the beginning was the Word.

When from the deeps of dying God astounded
Angels and devils who do all but die
Seeing Him fallen where thou couldst not follow,
Seeing Him mounted where thou couldst not fly,
Hand on the hilt, thou hast halted all thy legions
Waiting the Tetelestai and the acclaim,
Swords that salute Him dead and everlasting
God beyond God and greater than His Name.

Round us and over us the cold thoughts creeping
(Michael, Michael: Michael of the battle-cry!)
Round us and under us the thronged world sleeping
(Michael, Michael: Michael of the Charge!)
Guard us the Word; the trysting and the trusting
Edge upon the honour and the blade unrusting
Fine as the hair and tauter than the harpstring
Ready as when it rang upon the targe.

He that giveth peace unto us; not as the world giveth:
He that giveth law unto us; not as the scribes:
Shall he be softened for the softening of the cities
Patient in usury; delicate in bribes?
They that come to quiet us, saying the sword is broken,
Break man with famine, fetter them with gold,
Sell them as sheep; and He shall know the selling
For He was more than murdered. He was sold.

Michael, Michael: Michael of the Mustering,

Michael of the marching on the mountains of the Lord,
Marshal the world and purge of rot and riot
Rule through the world till all the world be quiet:
Only establish when the world is broken
What is unbroken is the word.

To the Unknown Warrior

You whom the kings saluted; who refused not
The one great pleasure of ignoble days,
Fame without name and glory without gossip,
Whom no biographer befouls with praise.

Who said of you "Defeated"? In the darkness
The dug-out where the limelight never comes,
Nor the big drum of Barnum's show can shatter
That vibrant stillness after all the drums.

Though the time comes when every Yankee circus
Can use our soldiers for its sandwich-men,
When those that pay the piper call the tune,
You will not dance. You will not move again.

You will not march for Fatty Arbuckle,
Though he have yet a favourable press,
Tender as San Francisco to St. Francis
Or all the angels of Los Angeles.

They shall not storm the last unfallen fortress,
The lonely castle where uncowed and free,
Dwells the unknown and undefeated warrior
That did alone defeat Publicity.

The Towers of Time

Under what withering leprous light
The very grass as hair is grey,
Grass in the cracks of the paven courts
Of gods we graved but yesterday.
Senate, republic, empire, all
We leaned our backs on like a wall
And blessed as strong and blamed as stolid--
Can it be these that waver and fall?
    And what is this like a ghost returning,
    A dream grown strong in the strong daylight?
    The all-forsaken, the unforgotten,
    The ever-behind and out of sight.
    We turned our backs and our blind flesh felt it
    Growing and growing, a tower in height.

Ah, not alone the evil splendour
And not the insolent arms alone
Break with the ramrod, stiff and brittle,
The sceptre of the nordic throne;
But things of manlier renown
Reel in the wreck of throne and crown,
With tyrannous tyranny, tyrannous loyalty
Tyrannous liberty, all gone down.

(There is never a crack in the ivory tower
Or a hinge to groan in the house of gold

Or a leaf of the rose in the wind to wither
And she grows young as the world grows old.
A Woman clothed with the sun returning
to clothe the sun when the sun is cold.)

Ah, who had guessed that in a moment
Great Liberty that loosed the tribes,
the Republic of the young men's battles
Grew stale and stank of old men's bribes;
And where we watched her smile in power
A statue like a starry tower
the stone face sneers as in a nightmare
Down on a world that worms devour.
 (Archaic incredible dead dawns breaking
 Deep in the deserts and waste and wealds,
 Where the dead cry aloud on Our Lady of Victories,
 Queen of the Eagles, aloft on the shields,
 And the sun is gone up on the Thundering Legion
 On the roads of Rome to the Battlefields.)

Ah, who had known who had not seen
How soft and sudden on the fame
Of my most noble English ships
The sunset light of Carthage came
And the thing I never had dreamed could be
In the house of my fathers came to me
Through the sea-wall cloven, the cloud and dark,
A voice divided, a doubtful sea.

(The light is bright on the Tower of David,
The evening glows with the morning star
In the skies turned back and the days returning
She walks so near who had wandered far
And in the heart of the swords, the seven times wounded,
Was never wearied as our hearts are.)

How swift as with a fall of snow
New things grow hoary with the light.
We watch the wrinkles crawl like snakes
On the new image in our sight.
The lines that sprang up taut and bold
Sag like primordial monsters old,
Sink in the bas-reliers of fossil
And the slow earth swallows them, fold on fold,
But light are the feet on the hills of the morning
Of the lambs that leap up to the Bride of the Sun,
And swift are the birds as the butterflies flashing
And sudden as laughter the rivulets run
And sudden for ever as summer lightning
the light is bright on the world begun.

Thou wilt not break as we have broken
The towers we reared to rival Thee.
More true to England than the English
More just to freedom than the free.
O trumpet of the intolerant truth

Thou art more full of grace and ruth
For the hopes of th world than the world that made them,
The world that murdered the loves of our youth.
    Thou art more kind to our dreams, Our Mother,
    Than the wise that wove us the dreams for shade.
    God if more good to the gods that mocked Him
    Than men are good to the gods they made.
    Tenderer with toys than a boy grown brutal,
    Breaking the puppets with which he played.

What are the flowers the garden guards not
And how but here should dreams return?
And how on hearths made cold with ruin
the wide wind-scattered ashes burn--
What is the home of the heart set free,
And where is the nesting of liberty,
And where from the world shall the world take shelter
And man be matter, and not with Thee?
    Wisdom is set in her throne of thunder,
    The Mirror of Justice blinds the day--
    Where are the towers that are not of the City,
    Trophies and trumpetings, where are they?
    Where over the maze of the world returning
    The bye-ways bend to the King's highway.

Tribute to Gladstone

Lift up your heads; in life, in death,
God knoweth his head was high;
Quit we the coward's broken breath,
Who watched a strong man die.

If ye must say "No more his peer
Cometh: the flag is furled,"
Stand not too near him; lest we hear
That slander on the world

The good green earth he loved and trod
Is still, with many a scar,
Writ in the chronicles of God
A giant-bearing star.

He fell: but Britain's banner swings
Above his sunken crown;
Black Death shall have his toil of kings
Before the cross goes down.

O young ones of a darker day,
In Art's wan colours clad,
Whose very love and hate are grey,
Whose very sin is sad,

Pass on: one agony long-drawn

Was merrier than your mirth;
When hand in hand came death and dawn
And spring was on the earth.

The Unpardonable Sin

I do not cry, beloved, neither curse.
    Silence and strength, these two at least are good.
    He gave me sun and stars and aught He could,
But not a woman's love; for that is hers.

He sealed her heart from sage and questioner --
    Yea, with seven seals, as he has sealed the grave.
    And if she give it to a drunken slave,
The Day of Judgment shall not challenge her.

Only this much: if one, deserving well,
    Touching your thin young hands and making suit,
    Feel not himself a crawling thing, a brute,
Buried and bricked in a forgotten hell;

Prophet and poet be he over sod,
    Prince among angels in the highest place,
    God help me, I will smite him on the face,
Before the glory of the face of God.

Variations of an Air

Old King Cole
Was a merry old soul
And a merry old soul was he
He called for his pipe
and he called for his bowl
and he called for his fiddlers three

after Lord Tennyson

Cole, that unwearied prince of Colchester,
Growing more gay with age and with long days
Deeper in laughter and desire of life
As that Virginian climber on our walls
Flames scarlet with the fading of the year;
Called for his wassail and that other weed
Virginian also, from the western woods
Where English Raleigh checked the boast of Spain,
And lighting joy with joy, and piling up
Pleasure as crown for pleasure, bade me bring
Those three, the minstrels whose emblazoned coats
Shone with the oyster-shells of Colchester;
And these three played, and playing grew more fain
Of mirth and music; till the heathen came
And the King slept beside the northern sea.

after W.B. Yeats

Of an old King in a story
From the grey sea-folk I have heard
Whose heart was no more broken
Than the wings of a bird.

As soon as the moon was silver
And the thin stars began,
He took his pipe and his tankard,
Like an old peasant man.

And three tall shadows were with him
And came at his command;
And played before him for ever
The fiddles of fairyland.

And he died in the young summer
Of the world's desire;
Before our hearts were broken
Like sticks in a fire.

after Walt Whitman

Me clairvoyant,
Me conscious of you, old camarado,
Needing no telescope, lorgnette, field-glass, opera-glass, myopic pince-nez,
Me piercing two thousand years with eye naked and not

ashamed;
The crown cannot hide you from me,
Musty old feudal-heraldic trappings cannot hide you from me,
I perceive that you drink.
(I am drinking with you. I am as drunk as you are.)
I see you are inhaling tobacco, puffing, smoking, spitting
(I do not object to your spitting),
You prophetic of American largeness,
You anticipating the broad masculine manners of these States;
I see in you also there are movements, tremors, tears, desire for the melodious,
I salute your three violinists, endlessly making vibrations,
Rigid, relentless, capable of going on for ever;
They play my accompaniment; but I shall take no notice of any accompaniment;
I myself am a complete orchestra.
So long.

Who Goes Home?

In the city set upon slime and loam
They cry in their parliament 'Who goes home?'
And there comes no answer in arch or dome,
For none in the city of graves goes home.
Yet these shall perish and understand,
For God has pity on this great land.

Men that are men again; who goes home?
Tocsin and trumpeter! Who goes home?
For there's blood on the field and blood on the foam
And blood on the body when Man goes home.
And a voice valedictory . . . Who is for Victory?
Who is for Liberty? Who goes home?

Wine and Water

Old Noah he had an ostrich farm and fowls on the largest scale,
He ate his egg with a ladle in a egg-cup big as a pail,
And the soup he took was Elephant Soup and fish he took was Whale,
But they all were small to the cellar he took when he set out to sail,
And Noah he often said to his wife when he sat down to dine,
"I don't care where the water goes if it doesn't get into the wine."

The cataract of the cliff of heaven fell blinding off the brink
As if it would wash the stars away as suds go down a sink,
The seven heavens came roaring down for the throats of hell to drink,
And Noah he cocked his eye and said, "It looks like rain, I think,
The water has drowned the Matterhorn as deep as a Mendip mine,
But I don't care where the water goes if it doesn't get into the wine."

But Noah he sinned, and we have sinned; on tipsy feet

we trod,

Till a great big black teetotaller was sent to us for a rod,

And you can't get wine at a P.S.A., or chapel, or Eisteddfod,

For the Curse of Water has come again because of the wrath of God,

And water is on the Bishop's board and the Higher Thinker's shrine,

But I don't care where the water goes if it doesn't get into the wine.

The Wise Men

Step softly, under snow or rain,
To find the place where men can pray;
The way is all so very plain
That we may lose the way.

Oh, we have learnt to peer and pore
On tortured puzzles from our youth,
We know all the labyrinthine lore,
We are the three wise men of yore,
And we know all things but truth.

We have gone round and round the hill
And lost the wood among the trees,
And learnt long names for every ill,
And serve the made gods, naming still
The furies the Eumenides.

The gods of violence took the veil
Of vision and philosophy,
The Serpent that brought all men bale,
He bites his own accursed tail,
And calls himself Eternity.

Go humbly ... it has hailed and snowed...
With voices low and lanterns lit;
So very simple is the road,

That we may stray from it.

The world grows terrible and white,
And blinding white the breaking day;
We walk bewildered in the light,
For something is too large for sight,
And something much too plain to say.

The Child that was ere worlds begun
(... We need but walk a little way,
We need but see a latch undone...)
The Child that played with moon and sun
Is playing with a little hay.

The house from which the heavens are fed,
The old strange house that is our own,
Where trick of words are never said,
And Mercy is as plain as bread,
And Honour is as hard as stone.

Go humbly, humble are the skies,
And low and large and fierce the Star;
So very near the Manger lies
That we may travel far.

Hark! Laughter like a lion wakes
To roar to the resounding plain.
And the whole heaven shouts and shakes,

For God Himself is born again,
And we are little children walking
    Through the snow and rain.

A Word

A word came forth in Galilee, a word like to a star;
It climbed and rang and blessed and burnt wherever brave hearts are;
A word of sudden secret hope, of trial and increase
Of wrath and pity fused in fire, and passion kissing peace.
A star that o'er the citied world beckoned, a sword of flame;
A star with myriad thunders tongued: a mighty word there came.

The wedge's dart passed into it, the groan of timber wains,
The ringing of the river nails, the shrieking of the planes;
The hammering on the roofs at morn, the busy workshop roar;
The hiss of shavings drifted deep along the windy floor;
The heat browned toiler's crooning song, the hum of human worth
Mingled of all the noise of crafts, the ringing word went forth.

The splash of nets passed into it, the grind of sand and shell,
The boat-hook's clash, the boas-oars' jar, the cries to buy and sell,
The flapping of the landed shoals, the canvas crackling free,

And through all varied notes and cries, the roaring of the sea,
The noise of little lives and brave, of needy lives and high;
In gathering all the throes of earth, the living word went by.

Earth's giants bowed down to it, in Empire's huge eclipse,
When darkness sat above the thrones, seven thunders on her lips,
The woes of cities entered it, the clang of idols' falls,
The scream of filthy Caesars stabbed high in their brazen halls,
The dim hoarse floods of naked men, the world-realms' snapping girth,
The trumpets of Apocalypse, the darkness of the earth:
The wrath that brake the eternal lamp and hid the eternal hill,

A world's destruction loading, the word went onward still--
The blaze of creeds passed into it, the hiss of horrid fires,
The headlong spear, the scarlet cross, the hair-shirt and the briars,
The cloistered brethren's thunderous chaunt, the errant champion's song,
The shifting of the crowns and thrones, the tangle of the strong.

The shattering fall of crest and crown and shield and cross and cope,
The tearing of the gauds of time, the blight of prince and pope,
The reign of ragged millions leagued to wrench a loaded debt,
Loud with the many-throated roar, the word went forward yet.
The song of wheels passed into it, the roaring and the smoke,
The riddle of the want and wage, the fogs that burn and choke.

The breaking of the girths of gold, the needs that creep and swell,
The strengthening hope, the dazing light, the deafening evangel,
Through kingdoms dead and empires damned, through changes without cease,
With earthquake, chaos, born and fed, rose,--and the word was "Peace."

Printed in Great Britain
by Amazon

33699533R00076